Southern Messenger Poets
DAVE SMITH, EDITOR

FOR LOVE OF COMMON WORDS

POEMS

Steve Scafidi

Louisiana State University Press)((*Baton Rouge*

Published by Louisiana State University Press
Copyright © 2006 by Steve Scafidi
All rights reserved
Manufactured in the United States of America
An LSU Press Paperback Original
FIRST PRINTING

DESIGNER: *Amanda McDonald Scallan* / TYPEFACE: *Whitman* / PRINTER AND BINDER: *Edwards Brothers, Inc.*

Library of Congress Cataloging-in-Publication Data

Scafidi, Steve.
    For love of common words : poems / Steve Scafidi
        p. cm. — (Southern messenger poets)
    ISBN 0-8071-3137-7 (pbk. : alk. paper)
    I. Title. II. Series.
PS3569.C247F67 2006
811'.6 — dc22

                                                                    2005016506

Grateful acknowledgment is made to the editors of the following publications, in which the poems listed first
appeared, sometimes in different form: *Blackbird,* "Calling to Her" (Fall 2002); *Mudfish,* "On the Texture of
Yewberries" (Spring 2005); *Shenandoah,* "Implement and Icon" (Spring 2004), "The Egg Suckers" (Spring 2005);
Kestrel, "The Fiddle and the Drum" (forthcoming); *Georgia Review,* "Ode to the Perineum" (Spring 2004).

Great thanks to Kathleen, Stephen, Sandy, Lisa, Katie, Nick, John Mark, Sue, and Paul.
A special thanks to Leslie Shiel for her abiding genius and her calm.

For Isabella Daria,
      Kathleen Kelly,
and the Grandparents

CONTENTS

ONE

Life Story of the Possible

At six in the evening on a Tuesday night
   after a supper of poached
      salmon and snails

Mr. Garland Calhoun, an ordinary bear
   eight foot tall with top hat,
      black tie and tails

unlatched the gate of his cage and walked
   the zoo quietly ambling
      under the silver trails

of the summer stars and his walking stick went
   tick-tock as he passed
      the zookeeper with his pails

and he passed the town clock and the library
   lit from inside and he passed
      the darkened jails

and he crossed the wooden bridge where the river
   passed beneath and sparkled
      with mica in the shale

and the dance hall was lit by blue lanterns made
   of paper so that you didn't walk in
      you sailed

and one hung so low from the ceiling it glowed
   like some miniature lucky
      moon from a fairy tale

and the bear finds his place by the bride and groom
   next to the clarinet player
      who is slender as a rail

and who smells of smoke and perfume and reads
   poetry at night alone
      in some kind of secret Braille

the fiddle player knows and now Garland Calhoun
   pulls two gold rings
            from his pocket with a nail

and the mermaid in the river combing her hair
  in the new darkness
           is just one more detail

of this day that is lost forever in the life story of
   the possible that is often
            pure loss and betrayal

and if Anne Frank is never to be a mother or to write
   another book or to dance
           with a bear in her white veil—

and she is not—then let this blue light hang down
  low like the soul
           of a world that failed.

River of Mirrors

The long sleek bass
　　bearded by the current
lays in the running
　　home the river is

and the river washes over
　　the fish and the force
helps to steady it
　　as it wavers slightly

still floating in place
　　in the rush of current
near a large stone jutting
　　up into the air where

a white sycamore branch
　　leans down gently
and among all the infinite
　　simultaneous details

of the world this one is
　　one too many to hold
suddenly and the idea
　　of god always suffers

and things fall apart and
　　moving very slightly
oblivious in its way
　　soon the fish is going

to be dragged out of
　　this habitat of speed
and rushing water that is
　　its wild green home

and be dashed against
　　the stone where leaves
of the sycamore curl
　　and someone with a line

in the water feels the pull
of something hidden
leap suddenly flashing
like a mirror in the sun.

Calling to Her

The Beauty Bush that never blooms waves
        in the yard and gods of all kinds die
every year of loneliness wandering down
into mountain valleys to look at themselves
in the Shenandoah or the Amazon and it's clear
        to all of us that you are not yet here.

Who knew we could need one more mouth
        to feed and to listen to and to love?
Lingerer, come on! Your mother and I
have already started to embarrass you
making love everyday. Every day this Spring
        we have called to you in the body's way.

Of calling that is careful and gentle
        we have invented three new ways!
Come on! Creature sprawled in the high
still trees of the jungle heaven must be,
wake up and swing down to us. Come on.
        I will buy you a seersucker suit.

Your mother will keep your favorite cigars
        in a mason jar and I will help sometimes
to encourage you when you mow the yard.
It is only three quarters of an acre but
we have twenty-nine redbud trees, wild
        raspberries and today I planted

the rooty burlap of a hemlock in the yard
        if you are homesick and need to climb
the high branches and look at the world from
some distance and remove both of which
we all need sometimes. I've written these lines
        to tempt you and your mother says

she loves you and it is true her eyes send light
           so warm and clear the sunlight you know
and are used to—you will find shining here
when she looks at you. Look! She is making
a sandwich with peanut butter and bananas.
           It is delicious. You'll love it. Come on.

What Rose Light as Breath

What tingling singing something
      moves to the very edges
            of my fingertips stings

sweetly and completely
      it is Spring and moths
            batter their new wings

against the dark warm air
      and they know something
            brighter than starlight is here

at last and blooms away
      in the garden's tiny square
            of wild green will

and look at the daffodils
      goddamn look at them
            we say walking in the yard

in the dark on the first warm
      night of April and cars nearby
            swerve out of control

and then head back into it
      as the loud long whew
            of strangers driving by

tonight sounds just like
      the world's relief that through
            the winter night's constant

cold this night has come
      and who knows how it gets here
            just in time to save us

from dying's dizzy liquor
      and the white eyes of potatoes
            staring in the cellar should win

the Nobel Prize for Dumb Luck
    while the bells of the verb *to be*
        ring-a-ding-ding calling us

to the holy dark of this first
    warm night of Spring where
        something is going full-speed

into the light of the next day
    that is not my birthday
        but should be someone's

birthday coming on and if enthusiasm
    implies love and joy and all
        the words I live for finding

fit synonyms for, then let it
    be known forever onward
        that on this night Kathleen

raised her arms and reached
    up into the sky and pulled
        my body down because

it was starting slowly to rise
    and even gravity itself,
        that always falling force

against which the world
    pushes and pushes gently
        rose light as breath.

Ode to the Middle Finger

Blunt eloquent digit—
it points to the sky
where Johnny Cash is
reunited with his bride
and his brother Jack
who died in the teeth
of a mill saw ripping
boards a long time ago
and the circle is at last
unbroken for Johnny Cash
who gave the finger to
the warden famously
once at Folsom Prison
singing to the citizens
there in 1968 and so
I also thank god for all
the rich blessings of
the middle finger which
the middle finger bestows
somehow on the giver
and even the redwood,
the mighty redwood tree
takes the shape of it.
Even the dandelion.
And Johnny Cash is
dead and gone today
and the bird he raised
remains a common thing
I thank god for giving me
everyday to raise here
with fury and love, Oh
lord let this be my prayer.

The Mountain in the River

It is a pointed chunk of granite
  one point five miles south from
the Castleman's Ferry Bridge
  at the middle of the river's span

and when we first start to swim
  in late Spring when the water is icy
quick and deep the rock lies five feet
  under the surface and I walk out

of my house with shorts and boots
  and nothing else and wander into
the river to find my pivot and do
  stand with one foot balanced there

on the point of the rock and lean into
  the current until my body finds the old
equipoise kites find serenely leaning
  into the April wind and with my nose

just above the surface and arms out
  I look south to the cold water's green
advance and balance there like a boy
  playing some silly game and stay

there for a half hour or an hour if
  it's very hot and strangers float by
on black innertubes drinking beers,
  pissing probably though they wave

and cars pass on the road screaming
  by and usually the sycamore leaves
flutter and minnows gather nearby
  as my stillness wavers and breaks

and holds while the Shenandoah river
  I divide heads to the sea and one river
dies there like all the rest and one remains
  cradled in the rock-a-by light of the valley.

The Boast

I am so good-looking even the angel of death
    follows me around step-stepping quiet
wherever I go

and I know it is only a matter of time until
    gravity takes over the business of being
and a worm wakes

in the bruised humus of my brain and the earth
    turns the same as the moment before
and breath's extravagant

finale ends and the spirit—if that word
    properly describes what will lift out of
my grotesque new husk—

will lift and lift up as now the drifting
    buzzards of my region lift on invisible
heavings of air

that come by everyday at about tree level
    and sway through the twiggy impossible
reaches constantly

as if some sublime proof of forever is going on
    and my labyrinthine sad grammar reflects
this event poorly

as I try to describe the things of the world
    accurately with a language that overpours
my sense of order,

and soon the day will be over everywhere
    and the moon will rise so full of light
a glow-worm

could write its dark memoir and you could see
    the angel of death, a little too perfumy,
under your window

with a banjo and a clean white shirt
    and a singing voice so beautiful it hurts
to hear your name.

After Homer's Catalog of Ships

The wish kiss, the list kiss, the take-it-or-leave-it
   missed kiss we live forever without, the all-day,
the go-away, the closer-closer-you-cannot-
   get-closer-but-try kiss, the I-don't-know-
who-you-are-or-why kiss of new love
   and the I-know-why-and-love-this kiss old
love practices in the hollow of a mattress,
   the tender-kiss you give to a child quietly
on a forehead, the father-kiss rare and lonely
   as diamonds and the mother-kiss gratefully
there and the uncle-kiss and the aunt-leaning-
   forward-in-her-perfumes-and-her-pearls,
the first kiss outside the house and the thrilling
   taste hours later and the last kiss I cannot
imagine though it comes and the Judas-kiss
   breath is giving and taking every second
and the tongue-roaming-troubadour-kiss,
   the in-and-out kiss, the swirling-fuck-me-
now kiss and the faraway-you-are-gone kiss
   I send to my dead and to my secret loves
lost in dream and miles, oh the moist, holy
   stolen kiss of a sudden inspiration one feels in
the wind or just inches from the beloved
   face of an old friend that is mostly the breath
of words, and the kiss of X's in long letters,
   the treasure-kiss, the I'm-about-to-kiss-
you kiss the eyes leave invisible and tiny as
   the blown-and-caught kiss but what is best
tastes mysterious and you want one all the time
   and the pillow-kiss of loneliness prepares us
for the real-kiss that kills us later burying
   our bodies in love's long storybook kiss
living is and the telling-kiss, the wedding-
   kiss and the money-kiss, the see-you-soon-
my-moon kiss, the marathon, the tight-lipped
   silly kiss, the nineteenth and eighteenth century
and so on back to the fishes kisses time tells,
   each one different enough that Neanderthal
kissing was a world away from Victorian

lips and the twenty-first-century kiss goes
like this catalog now goes further and further,
    and the old momentum-kiss that made us all
begin to begin is the mattering-kiss, the bless-
    kiss and the undressing all kissing gets to
leads to this and I imagine angry wild Achilles
    in the Achaean ship kissed his sword the way
today a pilot will kiss the hulk of a bomb before
    it drops away and that kiss leads to the other
subtle one of the spark inside it and the kiss of
    earth that is decimating and the kiss my wife just
gave me on the back of my neck will stay here
    all day like a tattoo and the easy kiss of rhyme
will also last all day so that if I could, I would
    kiss whoever wanted to in the dark I long for
and miss, the yes-kiss, the bliss-kiss, the lovely-
    lovely-this-kiss the world is right now, leaning to.

The Split-Second Star

The faraway dot of an airplane gleams
    in the wide blue sky.
Just so, baby. We blink and shine.

Habits of the North American Sasquatch

She walks to water loping low
   and leans and drinks a long time—
the river scooped a little in her hands.
   And her breasts hang down lightly
in the current's cold and she goes

climbing back up the hill-slope
   to fir trees and the twirling birds
rise like wind in her path turning
   slow and she goes to the cave
where he waits and they are gentle

all day and tear apart the rabbit
   he caught and the burrs matted
in her fur bite as she rolls over
   his body and moans and so
it seems that the still secret life of

this mountain is the body's delight
   and she wanders by our house
in the middle of the night, naked,
   her teeth glittering sharply,
and we see her sometimes walking

between the house and the shed
   swinging her arms under the moon
wearing only a fedora she found.
   My fedora with the small iridescent
feather in the brim. Well that is that.

This myth the world cannot subtract.
   Lady of the caves and the lakes.
Queen of the tabloids and muddy tracks.
   Sweet Ape of the Tri-State area.
Ghost of Emily Dickinson. Come back.

The Egg Suckers

To the snakes and the rats and the weasels
　who skulk and tunnel and dig underneath
the moon and the earth to find the shiny
　white ovum of their dreams lying there

warmed under the hen who coughs a little
　moving away in the darkness of the gold
hay and the dust of my chicken coop
　I say hello now from about fifty feet away

in my writing room at the beginning of Spring
　for you are the egg suckers, the midnight
takers-away, the despised and slinky
　snoopers, the geniuses of the world who

will be here when we are no more—
　you who move with such deliberation,
what you want eventually you get, hauling
　the precious cargo gently between your jaws

moving back down through the hole you dug
　cradling the egg, tonguing and sucking on
the white egg I was to gather and I was
　to eat and the poor hen with her one

eye wide open watches you come and go
　as she watches me reach my hand beneath her
in the morning and hold this small compact
　beautiful form up to the sun to admire

the subtle brown of the egg and the perfect
　religious fit of it in my palm and I roll it
across my kitchen table in the morning
　before I crack it open and pour the egg

into my skillet and fry it openly thanking
　the holiness of the hen, this exotic bird
roosting here whose children I eat everyday
　over-easy with black pepper and a spoon.

Lullaby for the Wolf

Galileo's mountains and Galileo's trees
   Galileo's rivers and Galileo's seas
all make the world I live in his
    to give and the moon is made of cheese.
There is a fish I have heard speaking

Finnish to the stars and a spoon
   between the seats in my father's car.
There is a gnome in a picture
   in a book somewhere and the bright
of the dark is the color of my hair.

Someone told me that a god died
   so we don't have to. And yet, look.
Just look at us. Nothing's fair—
   people screaming, the rides too rough.
And Death with his huff and his puff.

There must be an atom always burning
   somewhere—a mansion in the sky
to which we are returning. A place
   of real quiet, a bundle of straw
where the wolf lies down by the door.

Maybe this is what our words are for.
   To be a lullaby for death. To know
paradise in the nonsense of the poet
   and the scientist—to say some
theory of peace to the wolf who is law.

The Boy Inside the Pumpkin

At five hundred and thirty pounds it won the blue ribbon
         at the Frederick County Fair and because all such vegetables
are too bitter to eat something had to be done—

and it was decided to haul the pumpkin to the river and the boy
         inside the pumpkin meanwhile lay curled in the dark mash
while they rolled it to the edge of the tailgate and heaved it

to the ground and he must have been in there all spring and all
         summer and through the long hot hours must have grown
restless in the goop although he looked almost peaceful lying

naked by the river among the broken loaves and the seeds where
         the ambulance drivers stood on their knees amazed
beside the boy opening his eyes as the slow Potomac moved

to the Chesapeake bay and the ocean where the waves make
         their way to every coast in the world and the boy inside
the pumpkin lies quietly in this world like a fact of the unlikely

and the most unlikely things happen everyday in this world
         and we go on unchanged and a body was found
on a baseball diamond in Frederick Maryland last spring

wearing only a t-shirt face down with both arms underneath
         the body and the details are listed in the Metro Section
of the Washington Post and so when you read about the child

you learn he was only nine years old and had a faint birthmark
         the exact shape of Kentucky on the small of his back
and could talk like a duck when he wanted to and you learn

the most unspeakable things in the slender Metro Section
         of the Washington Post and it corrupts your sense
of the world to know how often the impossible happens upon us

without mercy and it is not the fit subject of poetry and it is
         offensive to redeem the horror of that boy's last hours
but I can't stop trying to salvage something from the murderous

and the poisonous and last spring some small ordinary blossom
        grew suddenly more gigantic everyday and the boy inside
the vine became the boy inside the pumpkin who became

a turning in the darkness no one noticed although for a week
        hundreds of people at the fair stroked the fat sides of
the pumpkin and were amazed and a boy leans up on his elbows

now in the moss beside the river and looks around bewildered
        and asks for his mother and his father and they are delivered
amazed and these things never happen. They happen everyday.

Pietà

Before she is turned away
   for the last time in the moment
before the new world begins
   harrowing her like a field

and the sun and moon disappear
   and the stars and the houses
suddenly become illustrations
   in a book no longer to be

believed burning to ashes—
   before the earth beneath her
rises up through her body
   slowly, every green cell

yellowing in the aftermath—
   just before this begins and
it begins constantly over
   and over in the secret nucleus

of mothers quietly humming
   at every second continuously
she breathes the odor of honey,
   his hair still the odor of honey.

TWO

To Lean like a Broom at the Gates

To sweep the bright threshold of hell with my body—
  to keep the archway clean,
      the gates oiled and polished shall be
        my vocation after life
          and if I am lucky
      enough to sweep the bright threshold of hell

once in the morning and once thoroughly at night,
  it will be sufficient and there will be time
      at last to read the books of poets I love
        who pass weeping by me,
          winking into hell
      for to be dead at all is the only definition

I observe of hell and any damnation and inventive
  torture for my soul will be a pleasure
      of immense proportions
        for to feel anything at all
          is better than the blank
      susurrus of nirvana or the company of angels,

so pour lead down my throat, pull my intestines
  out like rope and tangle my body
      in briars, but don't leave me there
        in the ground maybe to rise
          to some cloudy city
      hovering over the world. Let my body burn

to ashes and spread them around. Knowing we are here
  now is adequate bliss. So let me suffer
      and cry out my losses and the losses
        of those nearby and let me be
          of use—like this—
      sweeping the bright threshold of the given world.

The Lower Dove

FOR MR. BRIAN

Because it is tradition
   to eat a little cake
on one's birthday

and because his day
   followed Mother's Day
by just a weekend

he found on his bench
   at work a white cake
with pink frosted roses

and the sophisticated
   plastic mold of a heart
with doves on which

the word *mother* scrolled
   across pleasantly and
someone had written

just below the word
   mother another word
carefully with a marker

so the cake said sweetly
   Happy Mother's Day
Mothertrucker except

of course with an *f*
   and I love this word
the way I love life

and the plastic white heart
   with the worst profanity
scrawled gracefully

is now tacked to the wall
  here beside my bench
where visitors

accidentally read
  the delicate graffiti
and say nothing

usually and move on
  and the two large doves
are cast so well

one can see clearly
  to count all 45
white tiny feathers

of the lower dove—
  and a faux doily of fine
plastic filigree

frames this piece of crap
  I love for what it says
about the world that has

brought us here to kill us
  a condition for which
we are grateful often

wild to enjoy and to savor
  all the way through
to the darkest shade

of what has no proper name
  except one that is sacred
simple and profane.

On the Texture of Yewberries

Like jizm or the spew and the spray
        of such oils love makes so slick
and mercurial love in all its forms
           is this shiny essence hidden

in the compact red berries that dot
        the cemetery rush of yews growing
scraggled and haywire in almost
           every graveyard in Virginia

and the boxwood with its antique
        ghosty floating odor cannot compare
to the promise of the rich minuscule
           berries of the yew when it comes

to an idea of life after death or hints of
        sex and the raw luminousness
of the naked body and so finally
           when we go to join the ground's

disparate and dissolute party of ions
        and the shaggy roots of the yew
overtake what is left of our lives
           and the spindles of white bone

break apart in the claustrophobic dark
        of death, this berry guarantees
some seasonal small expression
           of the will-to-be, some tiny

invisible portion of who we are surges
        through the green body
of the yew blooming in the cold October air
           to make this luscious red morsel

for someone to squish between her fingers
        blushing for knowing the fine
human creams and the jetting up of love maybe
           in the texture of yewberries.

The Charwood Box

FOR ROD

After the fire arrived it stayed
  running back and forth for days
eating everything on the mountain
  even the winter snakes who rose
to the warmth and whose tender
  eyes scorched under the earth
and all that was left stood
  like black stumps and shoots
of char like hell in the beginning
  when the devil's city was just
an idea he kept to himself
  floating in heaven and so when
Mr. Crumb arrived to cut wood
  for something fine to build for
himself it was clear at last
  his mind was gone, his wife
was dead and his dog was done
  and he cut down the thickest
of the standing trees and milled it
  not knowing what he had until
the bright heart pine stunk like
  turpentine when the saw cut
and the planer blades spit char
  and his lumber was thick and kiln
dried by the forest fire and the box
  he built in which he would
one day fit himself was sooty
  and pitch dark in places under
the polish and in other places
  was golden and bold figures of
heartwood shot out from every
  direction like a sunburst and you
would be blinded to stare and you
  would stare and when finally
he was buried and the devil
  came to sit on his grave and then

the angel came to negotiate this
    and that and to sing Mr. Crumb lay
beneath them hidden peaceful
    lost forever in that beautiful thing.

Rainy Millionaire Morning

Never mind a hot fudge sundae or the rhythms
    of speaking into a fan and the long night's pan
you sizzle in in agony of love under the moon.

Never mind the pleasures of being sitting there now
    must certainly be and never mind the static passive
unconjugable forms of the verb *to die,* never mind.

Only mind the rain as it falls all day to the ground
    and seems to rise up as well to clouds that move
not at all from over your house and over my house.

Mind the way the rain makes a longing sound like
    unlikely, unlikely, unlikely as the amphibrach
of water smacks the roof and you think of horses.

Hundreds of them, thousands running over a prairie
    so closely packed and fast you wonder what it is
that makes them move. The clouds above so move.

You are a stranger to me and so are you and most
    my readers I hope but there is one who definitely
knows the angle of my nose, the sound of my voice.

She is getting married on this very rainy morning
    to a man I am still friends with and although
she kissed me once and it killed me, we are done.

She is why so far today I have wasted your time,
    I'm sorry, and why already this crude book lies
worth about nothing in a bargain bin somewhere.

If by chance a star falls from the sky into your
    open mouth like often on summer days a fly will
or you are killed before the end of this, I am sorry.

But you made it. And if I ever get a million dollars
    I will give it all to you and let these words now
be my binding legal promise to you in such a case.

Now, then. Every unlikely incarnadine day
   the sun sits still and far away and we turn like
fools waiting to die and love breaks us open

like expert children smashing piñatas I want to
   fill up with air like Superman and blow out
the wretched sun that says: *this leaf is green,*

this man and this woman, and I want to explode
   like a bang more possible and dangerous than
the first one the universe lately sadly burst from.

Pop Pop Pop

Because twizzling swift molecules of oxygen
              pop in your brain and give you
everything you need to breathe in and defy death
              breathe in and defy death.
                        I tell myself that
this day likely is the last I have left.

I tell myself the reasons for love are as large
              as the moon, but they are less:
the blue egg in a bird's nest and the letter O—
              how tiny are the reasons we have
                        for not letting go
of love—this slow catapult of the soul.

We have the one and the zero and they encode
              whole worlds of information and so
you can take off your clothes on the Internet
              in Norway and someone in Tokyo
                        tonight will know
that your name is Ingrid. His name is Sven.

Well then, Konichiwa ladies and gentlemen.
              Today I saw the web site of
the Knight Riders of the Ku Klux Klan who
              operate in Winchester Virginia
                        just 15.3 miles from here.
These citizens of the world. These paragons of purity.

Every night this week they come to Summit Point
              to paint their three ragged
malignant letters on everything they see—
              the stop signs, oak trees
                        and the dark blue of the street.
The letters are huge and the meaning is plain.

It is the twenty-first century. Paint comes in a can.
Sven and Ingrid are sleeping
by now in Oslo and several people watch
in Japan. You can live your whole life
here in America
and never learn how to love or how to be a man.

On the Death of Karla Faye Tucker

And why not celebrate the deaths of our enemies?
        Achilles dragging the corpse of Hektor
            through war fields of Troy
      sang a lost and hymnal cadence of joy
I imagine that warmed the cold hearts of the gods

for love of blood and vengeance and victory
        has always been a kind of prayer.
           Dante among the souls
      in hell's garden swooned to hear so many
tormented cries from the delicate blue mouths

of the damned and was full of sympathy at first
        which was blasphemy and he learned
           slowly to savor the terror
      of sinners and learned compassion only
goes so far and then must end and turn to an ugliness

without end which is hell. And so the idea of heaven
        must also be steeped in a cruelty
           without end. Why not
      then, celebrate the deaths of our enemies—
those who break into our lives without being asked,

to crush and to maim? For Texas just killed a woman
        who took a pick ax for a while against
           gravity and swung it
      down into the curled body of another
woman trying to sleep—just to sleep—one night

and who begged after a while more to be killed
        quicker and who was not. Why not
           raise a drink and sing
      when the murderer's arm swells up
darkly and the brain stops and her shining soul

plummets into whatever abyss her god invented
      meticulously and patiently one night
            raking over the coals
      of His own—I suppose—mysterious
rages and childhood dementia and darkness old

as His gods which are the coals themselves twinkling
      like starlight here in America where
                  what is commonly
      unspeakable is frequently described—
a thing by which we might recognize ourselves. No,

I can't celebrate the death of Karla Faye Tucker
      although I would like to. Although
                  I have tried.
            So goodbye ax. Goodbye stars.
Goodbye gods we make to sanction who we are

but will not now admit—simple thugs of history
      we are given today to alter somehow
                  for our own sake.
            Even the bloody Achilles eventually
gave Hektor's body to Hektor's father at the gate.

Lord, I give you back your image and the myth
      of benevolence and the illusion
                  You exist.
            Karla Tucker was not my enemy.
Horror is. That common murderous evil bitch.

For My Friend Todd Hardy Who Says We Die and That's It

And Jimi Hendrix who seems to say the opposite everyday
                     with his guitar
          I dedicate these words written in May
                     2005 to mark the end of the arguments
          we have about the meaning of life and
                     what happens to us after we die.

For you'd think it would be enough to carry your body
                     slung loose
          and broken at your side and go down
                     to the door and walk through. But no.
          Thousands of years continue, Todd says,
                     without you and it is not enough to die.

You must disappear completely and all signs be obliterated
                     and the mind
          tries to protect us from knowing this
                     and well, thank you but it's easy
          to see through the white veil of invention
                     and imagination to the sad grave

heaving of nothing that is waiting and my friend Todd Hardy
                     says we die
          and that's it and I'd like to argue
                     some dark spooling out of fabric with
          an embroidered bear walking along
                     the mountain pass between this life

and some other and point out the burrs matted there
                     in the bear's fur
          and the beehive full of honey in the green
                     pine she is about to climb but the mind knows—
          it knows about death and how all faith
                     is our commitment to a guess

and my friend Todd Hardy who collects 8-track cassettes
                     of Jimi Hendrix
          and the wrecked psychedelia of heroic
                     guitars ruins my hope that we might live on

somehow in the spinning of an atom or
                a compact disc or the dusty fur of a bear.

Well, my friend, you win. Soon we will not even have been
             the dust of dust
disappearing and in ten thousand years
         even that dust will enter the maw
of an oblivion I cannot put my faith in. So,
              let the sacred guesswork begin.

Witness to the Work

If I could knock a house down with my crotch or pull a train
   cross-country with a little string tied to my cock well then
that would be something. Not much, but at least something.

If I could breathe in sharply now and swallow the western half
   of Portugal with its bright umbrellas and pointy cathedrals
and its statues of Fernando Pessoa it might be the same.

If I could just think of the pain I would fall over like a lettuce.
   As it is, a great and growing awe comes between us now
and we do not speak of it. Months pass. More months.

She cries out suddenly and her cries are deep like nothing
   I've ever heard and the car zigzags and we are there.
Then the hours pass filled with a difficult kind of grace.

And she pushes that baby out of her and the baby finally
   says OK and galumph, just like that, this lump of breath
falls into the world and is lifted to her mother's breast.

And she is crying and people are snipping and cutting, saying
   Oh isn't she, isn't she and the room is spinning hard
and this spinning spins the earth and the earth spins faster.

And I always thought that life was like a blue donkey
   named Disaster that we ride to death and whisper to.
Now I know. It is this bloody holy work the mothers do.

The Meeting Place

This large green hill
   takes the whole page
except for the corners

at the top left and right
   which are two triangles
of blue sky one darker

than the other by a degree
   or two of night coming on
or the day just beginning

in the book of photographs
   so oversized it looks like
I am carrying a small door

open in front of me as I walk
   out into the backyard
thinking of you and this hill

seems a perfect place to meet
   in case we are separated
which of course we will be

from our friends and family
   which is why this poem
should be folded gently

tucked into your pocket
   so that you'll find a way
to the house on the left

of the hill where inside
   it's warm and dolphins
leap across the wallpaper.

At the Tomb of the Unknown Soldier

The beautiful inappropriate laughter
    of a boy about seventeen—
his white bones lost in the dark of his body.

Implement and Icon

There is a shiny pitchfork hovering vertically
  in the air among the trees on the hill here
in the country my mind has become and the tines—

three steel prongs about twelve elegant
  inches long—point to the blue sky and the oak
handle is worn dark in two places from use.

At dusk when the sun lowers and the mountains
  rise up the fork begins slowly to burnish
to a deep red but otherwise is unremarkable.

It simply floats iconic as a statue of Mary
  in a pilgrim's mind and does no real harm
standing as an image or a symbol in the woods.

Deer come up to it and sniff the handle wary
  and walk away. Birds perch on the pointy
tips awkwardly singing and then fly away.

I've needed to write about this for a long time—
  this pitchfork motionless here in the mind—
full of rage these days, full of murderous rage.

For example with my mind humming last night
  in the dark at the end of my drive I waited
for the teenage vandals to crush my mailbox

for the third time in two weeks and hoped
  to god they'd stop and climb out of their car
nervous and giggly so I could wreck whatever

their mothers loved in them and walk back up
  the drive covered in the gore of my feelings.
For example a missile now tearing up the blue.

Or a car swerving into you on the highway.
  For example what eventually crosses
your mind standing at that pit in Manhattan.

Murder must be the refuge of the oldest rage
for this pitchfork floats on my green hill
like a god. So peaceful, this icon of the Age.

Where We Work

Upstairs is Bill and Chip and Lucy and Carol and Jeff
  and downstairs Little Bill, Mike, Hot Toddy, John Mark,
Mr. Brian and me and in the stripping room is Jack and
  Matt who is new and Nick runs up and down the stairs
and in between us and in the muddy field across the way
  is the donkey and the mule and six African geese, eight
ducks, one rooster, and a golden hen and up the drive is

the henhouse Ghorley repaired and in the pasture behind
  the barn groundhogs build tunnels and raise their young
and stand up to see what is going on and underneath
  the barn where we work and which leans 10 degrees south
lives a skunk white and huge without the black stripe and
  there is wind and snow and heat like most places and trucks
and cars parked higgledy piggledy and the stock tank full

of goldfish starving and two cement deer with purple eyes
  made of glass stand by and someone who died left them here
for us and the land goes on for acres until the behemoth
  new homes wreck it along the borders and everyday it seems
they sail closer like the ships of a terrible country that has
  sent emissaries to us who have our own customs and traditions
and this is as close to heaven on earth as I expect to find

and this is just a barn built of oak in the 1930s and the days
  pass one after another as usual and what I forgot to include
goes on forever and includes Kevin in New Orleans, Chris
  in Manhattan and seven ravens in the willow and the wounded
scatter of cats, the eighteenth-century Chippendale chairs,
  chisels honing, and the carving of the finial of a pine clock,
and the amazing genius of bullshit and laughter and a cloud

floating by in the April sky with darkness at the bottom and
  lightning inside like a city moving a hundred miles per hour
over us and someone standing by a door pointing at the sky
  and the donkey, suddenly speaking for us, says it all just fine.

To an Old Woman in the Air

As you fly over my grave
      with your jet pack on turbo
            to play bingo in Fargo—

as your children lift up
      their children to point
            at the nearby moon tonight,

as you travel toward us
      who lay lost in death—
            think of your mother now

sleeping with you upstairs
      think of your father asleep
            on the sofa with a work-book

propped on his bony knees
      think of the small overlooked
            details of who we were once.

Your mother's golden bangs
      almost cut in a straight line
            that she trimmed with scissors

earlier in the round mirror
      by the kitchen where water
            cooked in the tea kettle,

and my fingertips stained dark
      walnut from working all day.
            Think of the way your body

wiggled in the bath an hour ago.
      You are older now than I ever was.
            I am guessing you have suffered.

I am hoping days of unexplained
      joy ambushed you at every turn
            and that your life is saturated

with the secret water of days
that will always be just a part
of a larger water more powerful

than the Shenandoah beside
which your mother and I lived
before you were born. I hope

the river of your days rushing by
grows more graceful as you age.
I hope as you fly over our grave

today with your jet pack on low
the day is bright and clear
and the traffic through the trees

is just sparrows and leaves. Old
woman, I can hear you calling
and your mother turning to you

right now. This instant. We are all
awake now. We are long gone.
Baby, Old Lady, Go on.

THREE

For Love of Common Things

The heaven trees jump out of the ground everywhere
        all at once along train track and fence line
            and no one likes a trash tree
        soft of wood, dumb of grain, murderous
to the useful trees that suffer growing slowly beneath

their canopy of branches and for this I have learned
        to prize them—the country palm
            the paradise tree
        the sweet and maligned ailanthus
no good for burning or turning or building a thing

and so I have planted a small grove in the back
        that will tower over my dilapidated
            faded shed and will crack
        in the first ice because of their inherent
weakness and they will not die but spread everywhere

like a talus of the human spirit for it's not the strong
        who survive mostly but the determined
            the ugly and the lucky,
        and a friend once built a fence of ailanthus
cutting the trees into sticks and making a low garden wall

one winter and by the spring every post was sprouting
        unaccountably into a living green wall
            of defiance and I imagine
        Eden was wild with poison ivy and miles of
kudzu and the lake teemed with crocodiles and the great

poet Czeslaw Milosz died today and now wanders I hope
        among the paradise trees of the beautiful
            Lithuanian quarter of
        heaven where one is allowed to question
and grow doubtful and argue with friends and smoke

and if there is a heaven of any kind Oh lord let it be
this city where the poet undresses
tonight and swims
in the river while the mermaid plays
a ukulele and calls to him under the silver trees.

Lullaby for the Lamb

The wishbone snaps! A woman's lap
    and a million dollars in cash collapse.
This is the day good luck attacks
    and sweetness comes to crack your back.
Here is a monkey with a paw attached.

I've got a knack for the zig and the zag
    and keep a thousand words for love
each in a sack. I'm a tiny haystack
    burning in the twilight as a white bird
circles and circles. The moon just drags

the sun around and Death is in you like
    a thumbtack. You have to pull things
from your ass—and say so. All ghosts
    go rickety-rack like trains to Ohio
when it snows. Mother's milk just goes.

Therefore, drink up, child. Drink up.
    The world is like a slaughterhouse
and Being is the lamb. Soon you will
    understand the blah-blah back-beat
of blessings and be at home in the world

we are probably messing up for you
    almost completely. I have witnessed
any number of beautiful things falling
    from the sky. Gently into our hands.
Here is your mother and your fatherland.

Elegy for Jam Master Jay

Oh this squelchy sound rises scratching through the air
            back and back and then back and forth
and the sound sticks with you like a hickey
            going wicky-wicky loud and swiftly
and no sound on earth is more appropriate to
            the rickety green wind of a summer day
                in this West Virginia

where my town is so quiet even the sparrows
            move hushed through heavy green leaves
of the oaks and the children all nap on their arms
            stretched out on their beds dreaming
while the sunlight in ticker tape rays is streaming
            and the kitchen knives and the kitchen forks
                sleep in the shaded dark

of the kitchen drawers of all the houses here
            in Summit Point where quiet is the law
of the garden and the pathway curving toward
            a blossoming seed breaking under ground
from which soon a red pepper will burst into flames
            and so the fingers of the dj play
                the turntable slowly

on the record I turn up today so the whole town
            can hear the wicky-wicky sound
of Jam Master Jay going back and back—
            back and forth repeatedly and serenely
behind the glorious raps of Run-DMC
            who rose out of New York City to say
                a wilder poetry

still more new than mine or my contemporaries
            who do not trust enough the rhymes of
true clear nights and the playful old beat-box
            rhythm of days and Master Jay
is dead now and his fingers are lost in the grave
            force that mixes making everything
                move with grace.

To Women Bathing in Distant Cities

Donkey-eared man of the mid-Spring moon!
  Fool I am. Boss of the moss on the stone
colored stones of the creek behind my home.

  Slow horse of a man. Millionaire of want.
Every night I do nothing and write long
  erotic letters to a woman I do not know,

have never met and yet dream of her naked
  tits hanging from her and the black bush
hidden from view and every night I call to her

  I call to you and celebrate the profane terms
of the body that are a trillion-fold of tenderness
  and lovely as music—her Cello, her Beatrice,

her Basket of Loaves and Fishes, her Seaside
  Hotel, her Wishing Well and the Catacombs
of Ancient Rome, Grove, Grotto, Honeycomb

  of Pleasure and Beginnings. I hear the lucky
guitar of being here breathing gently strums
  and my Newport Flowering Pear blossoms

here under the May moon, my Come Along
  Way, my Miles to Go Before I Sleep, Oh my
Deep-Voiced Caballero, my Wheelbarrow.

  We have a whole variety of nuts for the balls.
The words *wang* and *woo*. We have the Louvre
  and tight summer night Mona Lisa halls.

Oh women bathing in distant cities washing
  there in the quiet study of your quiet room,
I think of you without looking listening

  to the world outside. Leaning back. Oh
we should have some secret pass-phrase
  brokered here between us that means

nothing to anyone else and something fine
   to the woman I am thinking of who knows
love by the body's slang and the body's rhyme.

In Praise of Myron Walker's Buttons

In the age of the fedora and the pocketwatch
   two young men sat in the early morning crush
of hurry that breakfast in the diner often was

and this day was the first day for Myron Walker
   as a salesman of encyclopedias in New York City
and my friend's father told him this story I love

for Myron suddenly needed to go to the bathroom
   before leaving for the door-to-door work of the day
already nervous and sweaty and puffing the air

and frantic inside with worry for his new wife and
   his beautiful child at home where everything
was threadbare but his new suit which because

of the purgative effect of the coffee and the strain
   of life he soiled on his brief walk to the toilet
and this was the first day at work so he cleaned

himself with tap water splashing in that dim little room
   and when he returned to the front booth by the door
Mr. Edwin Greer smelled something difficult exactly

to believe until he saw all of the white buttons
   of Myron's suit shine with his good work except
in those four little ovals where the thread holds

the button to the cloth, each of which was full of
   excrement and so with shit in his buttons Myron
knocked on the doors of the citizens of Brooklyn

and made no sales and cried and walked home
   that night learning to live with his failure which
was thorough and intricate although temporary

and when Nick tells this story amazed we laugh
   at Myron Walker and we love him and we are glad
to have company in our foolishness which is deep

and our dignity which frankly fluctuates according
to the cruelty of things and our lives are renewed
here in the time of the ball-cap and the Velcro shoe.

The Fiddle and the Drum

FOR SUE AND PAUL

Frost killed every bloom on the Beauty Bush
        last night and now there is no way to describe
the pink embellishment of the April sky and yet
            Spring is here and my old joy blooms in the world.

Inside this century everyone I know is going to die!
        A man is kissed tonight in the Virginia Penitentiary
and rhymes are trivializing everything nearby
            for the poor sake of music and the reader's heart.

My sister's college roommate said she heard a ghost
        once quietly fart and I didn't think such a thing
was audible but apparently a cricket rubs its legs
            together when it sings and anything is possible.

Ghosts must wander the hallways of every hospital
        and every street of every city in the world must be
a white blurry pageant of sorrow and of chains.
            Maybe one of them has a little drum. Maybe

another has a fiddle and somewhere in death
        they play and a crowd of the dead somewhere
sashay. Sashay! Today I woke up for no reason
            smiling like Saint Francis suffering dementia

and called the birds in my mind and administered
        to the poor in my heart who gather like the birds
who gather like the words I love starved for love
            which darts and weaves and is still

my favorite word the way Joseph and Mary's third
        anonymous child who died at birth was theirs,
her hair so bright you can still see that deep brief
            blaze of light moving under your skin.

Lines for a Doorway

The Shenandoah disappears where it converges in the flow
        of the Potomac ten miles from here
                and nothing Shakespeare ever said
                        sticks in my ear like *hello,*

my love when I get home so pity the beauty of art
        and pity the monument
                to grace a river is as it goes
                        slowly without forethought to

the green grave of the sea and pity the moon dented
        by the white boots of astronauts
                and look—look at the sun
                        rolling overhead like a wheel

and wherever we go after death is OK with me
        as long as death comes too
                eventually and the sentimental
                        X's crossed over the eyes

of everyone who has already lived imply an alphabet
        that spells nothing but sorrow
                which is exactly why
                        when I get home ruined

from work and the moon disintegrates from the light
        friction of its voyage
                in the cold dark of space
            she says *hello there, my love* and touches my face.

To a Girl on a Broken Porch

There really is no good reason for being alive—
            It is as you say
                        pointless, brief and mean
and yet that is the beauty
            of discovering suddenly a slug
all night while you slept wrote something

indecipherable and silvery in trails across
            the screen door and so what
                        if you are ugly
and no one loves you. For you will die
            one day as I will
eventually and you are absolutely right.

It hurts like a motherfucker and has no real
            intrinsic meaning and so
                        we are doomed. Very well.
Consider the broom. Of all objects of grandeur
            and power it is devoid of
the least and devoted to floors and to muck.

And yet consider the broom! How beautiful
            the pine handle rises straight up
                        out of the yellow stalks
tied together in a tight stiff triangle
            of straw and string.
There is no good reason for anything, and yet

breathing sweeps through the body urgently
            and patiently. Sometimes
                        to be here at all is very
small and living requires this least amount
            of effort from you who are
perhaps a genius and a dashing specimen

of wit and charm without whom the world
is not worth sustaining
or celebrating tonight
as now that same slug on my screen door
celebrates the same world
making beautiful useless loopdeloops of slime.

Creature of puberty, shame and possibility
you are having a hard time
and I'm not being helpful.
Forgive me. That time was hell. I know.
No matter how long you live—
at the end your life will have been too brief.

So let this thing sweep through you slowly.
It affirms and persists.
It hurts like a motherfucker.
I don't know how else to do this. Who does?
We are all making it up as we go.
Whatever it is let it sweep through you. Slow.

The Language of Nomads and Ghosts

FOR LESLIE

Because names make the earth my home
    I love the sounds by which we are known—
Rodriguez and Stacy and Mr. John Holmes

    and the names for things around us—
the oak and the papaya and the xylophone
    and how it happens when you say "Hey,

I'm walking to the store for an ice cream,
    my darling, and do you want one too,"
how suddenly the anonymous blocks of

    brick become the jewelry shop on 5th,
Sam's Deli, H&H Realty, and O's Grocery
    and you walk, or, as *The American*

Heritage Dictionary of the English Language
    says, you "roam about in visible form
as a ghost" to the place where the sweet

    legacy of the Fourth Earl of Sandwich cools
and grab two of these dark arrangements
    by which two slabs of one material hold

a slab of another material between them
    and in this case two sugary black breads
together hold the icy milk of an animal

    raised since the beginning of time by
my ancestors and yours in the primitive
    Neolithic fields where we toiled once

traveling from one place to another
    in time which is defined by sorrow and
"the continuum in which all events occur

in apparently irreversible succession
from the past to the present to the future"
and you walk home and roam the world

all alone like a nomad or a ghost in the city
with the outline of chocolate on your lips,
all our dark sweet words at your fingertips.

Ode to the Perineum

Maybe the soul is only a small place on the body.
                    —LARRY LEVIS

And maybe not. Maybe the invisible filament that flickers
            in the idea of the soul is the soul.
                    Some hummingbird of the universal mind—
brightly colored, precise and infinitely quick.

And dull. It shouldn't be, in any case, as intimate
            as say, the perineum, that pleasurable
                    one millionth acre
of nerves that lies between the asshole and the valleying

gradual beginning of our sex. No, the soul can't be that
            close by and so inappropriate
                    that to speak of it now
is to cross over into the language of the body and of

the hidden crevasses of the body. Well, the hummingbird
            now floats over a rose although
                    such a symbol for the soul
to be honest must include the microscopic blue turds

thudding lightly onto the grass wherever that hummingbird,
            for you, will pass. I prefer the t'aint,
                    this prairie of pure desire
so secret even the body knows little of its power until quietly

reminded we buck like a horse on some Mississippi street.
            This deep true south of ourselves.
                    Patch of the promised land.
Kingdom of the cartwheel and the lazy falling handstand

in swimming pools. I praise the carnival hairs sprouting
            there like trees Dr. Seuss drew
                    in a forbidden mood
and I praise blue moons, kazoos and white-hot rivers

with fiery canoes in that vision of scramble pleasure
    makes us live through and I praise
            this small place on the body
that might be the soul. Hinge from which our legs swing.

Tingling thing. Like the soft spot on a baby's head,
    this fragile holy span,
            must be praised now and then
with all the gentle force that words can stand.

To the Visiting Missiles of Who

Sunlight tings off the tin roof and flies back into space!
        Hippity-hey you can't catch me say
boy-birds to the girl-birds in a very arrogant
        insouciant way. In my town today
a thousand birds darken the sky in a wobbly shape
        of a paisley drape hung on a line to dry.
They swoop and they drop and they call their names.
        They swoop today and fall and say:
I'm Richie, I'm Susan, I'm Russell, I'm Tim, O hey,
        I'm Cedrick, I'm Ruth and so it begins
with sparrows that fall to the earth. Just sparrows.
        The sky's feathery arrows, these joyful
quicklings moving in a mob. Ever since September
        it seems that everything flying falls.

And now I think of the bomb and the ruin of all,
        the fiery sun that flattens a city,
the fiery city we saw. It makes my heart a hearse.
        Dread comes like a rhyme and a curse.
It zigzags to verse and hopes there is a way
        to stop the falling, the might of the drop—
the pop. Now an ant walks across my hand as I write.
        It crosses the page and it stops. Aah.
I breathe on it gently, it hops. I breathe, it hops.
        I breathe it walks. I blow and it hops and hops.
It knows the dark of underground rooms. It knows
        of fire and brooms. It knows who we are
and the missiles of boo, the missiles of loss, the missiles
        of whistles, the visiting missiles of who.

Tonight my mind is a drum. All dumb, dumb dumb.
        Whoever sets off the ruin of words,
the ruin of all that stands and turns, the ruin of all
        my mountains and the plashy dithyrambic
rhythm of fountains, I'm telling you now you'll fail.
        Whoever you are, you'll fail. Tonight
what swims in my wife swishes its glorious tail.
        You who will try and kill us one day,
remember the moo and the cow and the spoon.

Remember your mother and the billions
of others. We are all murderous too, so blind
reckless and frail. We fire like guns
and we might be the ones, but I'm telling you
now you'll fail. You'll fail. Whoever
you are, you will fail.

The Shimmy

Our brief time in the world—
    like a breast just popped from a dress
while the tipsy bride shimmies.

To My Infant Child on a Winter Night

On the night you were conceived some divine hand appeared
and now look at the magical starry fist coming toward us
like an asteroid icy and terrible in the night sky.

Little Fig, Little Onion-Headed Something Bundled in My Arms,
look to where your father reaches up to the sky pointing.
So we are all going to die. Well, big whoop.

You just gaze up from the swaddling of my arms and hiccup
suddenly and you do not cry. For such eloquence you are
beloved and you should know that the beloved

are marked and loss is like breath when one is marked.
For we will not die by what comes at us wild suddenly
from the midnight sky and we will not die from

words or what shines from a father's mind and yet we will—
Little Drifter into Dream—like our family before us, die
of old age and the chemicals in drinking water

and from the wearing down of bone joy eventually turns out
to be—for such is the burden of the beloved who arrive
astonished falling from our mothers' bodies.

I hope you learn to take the pointed counsel of the horsefly
and the bumblebee and your father's mind one day soon
and learn to sting the fat ass of the world that

wants us dead buried quietly in the world's grief and I hope
you learn to lean into whatever comes at you and learn
to take it and to take it on. Remember the great

fighter Muhammad Ali outsmarted George Foreman in 1974
by taking punch after punch one night in Zaire and so
when your sorrow comes take it. Rope-a-dope

loss and break it. Child, do this—watch—make a small tight fist
and shake it at the sky. The night is an idiot and blind, bigger
than your mother and I and we defy it with you

and this is really no way to welcome you to the shimmering
   lilac of being here but talking like this is all I know.
         Just a moment ago under the winter sky

you put your whole left hand right in my mouth and laughed
   and whatever hurtles from the sky now hurtles still
         and we will take it. Garbanzo of the Beautiful,

gazing up and looking at the world, I love how you hiccup
   quietly and stare. How you laugh when I joggle you
         in my arms and growl gently like a bear.

Through the Endless Streets of My Town

Because the King of West Virginia has decreed
          no more working long hours for nothing anymore
and no more card playing or sorrows, we are free

and after walking all day we sit in the tall grass
          just north of town where the orchard meets the pasture
smoking our Chinese pipes and laughing

for we have walked all day through Summit Point
          past the clock factory burned to its foundations,
past the stock exchange where the businessmen

howl and jabber eating popcorn from striped bags
          and we saw the procession of young bright women
marching up Church Street quietly toward the library

and we followed a white dog who skittered sideways
          to the aquarium where there is an octopus from
Madagascar hanging in the blue water of the tank

like a ghost with her arms going back and forth
          in the slow motion of dream and we have been
walking all day which is a motion like dream

and later Norman says he is going to float up over
          the orchard and look through the little windows
of sunlight on all of the apples and tell me what is

going on in that enormous city blossoming beside us
          as smoke rises from our long carved pipes
and in the meanwhile we have our sandwiches

and the horses of the imagination graze everywhere—
          real horses with names like Firelight, Old Spear,
Lucky Day, Hucklebuck, and My Blue Heaven Is Here.